GAME DAY

MATCH POINT

by David Sabino
illustrated by Setor Fiadzigbey

Ready-to-Read

SIMON SPOTLIGHT
An imprint of Simon & Schuster Children's Publishing Division
New York   London   Toronto   Sydney   New Delhi
1230 Avenue of the Americas, New York, New York 10020
This Simon Spotlight edition August 2020
Text copyright © 2020 by Simon & Schuster, Inc.
Illustrations copyright © 2020 by Setor Fiadzigbey
For information about special discounts for bulk purchases, please contact Simon & Schuster Special Sales
at 1-866-506-1949 or business@simonandschuster.com.
Manufactured in China 0520 LEO

GLOSSARY

ACE: A serve that wins a point without the opponent touching the ball

ALLEY: An area along both sides of the court that's used for doubles

BACKHAND: A stroke where the back of the hand points toward the direction of movement, with the arm crossing the body. For example, this stroke is used to return tennis balls that are hit to the left side of a right-handed player (and to the right of a left-handed player).

BASELINE: The back line of the court

BREAK POINT: When the receiver (person not serving) is one point away from winning a game while the opponent serves, they have a break point. When the server loses the game, the receiver has "broken" their serve.

DEUCE: When the score of a game is tied at 40–40

DOUBLES: A game of tennis played between two teams of two people who are most often of the same gender

DROP SHOT: When a player hits the ball and it lands very close to the net on the opponent's side

FAULT: A serve not in play

FOREHAND: A swing that begins with the racket to the side of a player's body. "Forehand" could also be used to describe a player using their dominant hand to play.

GAME: The first player to get four points wins that game. Players switch serving after each game.

LET: When the serve hits the net but lands in the service box. The serve is not considered a fault and can be replayed.

LOVE: Zero points

MIXED DOUBLES: A game of tennis played between two teams of two people. Each team contains one man and one woman.

OPEN ERA: The time beginning in 1968 when professional players were allowed to compete in major tournaments with amateurs

OUT: Any ball that lands out of the court of play

RALLY: When players hit the ball back and forth to each other

SERVE: The start of a point. One player hits the ball to their opponent over the net and into the service box from behind the baseline.

SET: A group of games in a match. To win a set, a player usually needs to win six games. To win a match, a player usually needs to win two or three sets.

SET POINT: When a player needs one more point to win a set

SINGLES: A game of tennis played between two people

SMASH: A hard shot that bounces high because it is hit straight down onto the opposite side of the court. This is also referred to as an overhand shot.

VOLLEY: A shot that is returned before it hits the ground

Hello! My name is Serena, and tennis
is my favorite sport.
My parents love tennis so much
that they named me after the
famous tennis player Serena Williams!
She is one of the best players in the world.

Millions of people watch tennis around the world.
That makes it one of the most popular sports on the planet.
Nearly eighty million people of all ages play tennis.

Today I am working at a big tennis tournament. A tournament is when people play many tennis matches to see who wins. I'm a ball girl. My job is to get the loose tennis balls and give them back to the players.
Do you want to come with me?

Here is the tennis center where I am
working today.
Inside there are ten tennis courts.
Some tennis centers have many
more courts, and others have fewer.

The USTA Billie Jean King National Tennis Center in New York City has twenty-two tennis courts inside, and more outside. That's where the best players in the world play in a special tournament called the US Open.

Wherever you go, tennis courts are always shaped like rectangles.
All are the exact same size.
But guess what? They can be made of different things like grass, clay, or even concrete.

When tennis is played on grass, it is called lawn tennis!
Clay courts are red or brown.
What kind of tennis courts do you think we have in this center?

Before we head over to the courts,
let's visit the locker rooms where
the players get ready for their matches.
This is my friend Donna.

Donna is all dressed for her game:
she's wearing shorts, a T-shirt, and of
course, tennis shoes.
Do you see what she has on her wrists?
Those are called sweatbands.
Donna uses those to wipe her face
when she is playing.

The other thing Donna needs for her game is a tennis racket.
The frame of a tennis racket can be metal, or a special composite material. The strings can be made from strong, light threads like nylon.

Look down by the courts!
Many people are waiting to ask the
players for autographs on tennis
balls. They get the balls at the
souvenir store in the tennis center.

Some stores at tennis centers sell
giant tennis balls so there is room
for many players to sign.
These stores also sell clothing,
rackets, books, shoes, and everything
else anyone needs to play tennis.

Large covers, called tarps, are put over the grass courts when it rains. Tarps help keep the courts dry and clean so they will be safe for the players to play on.

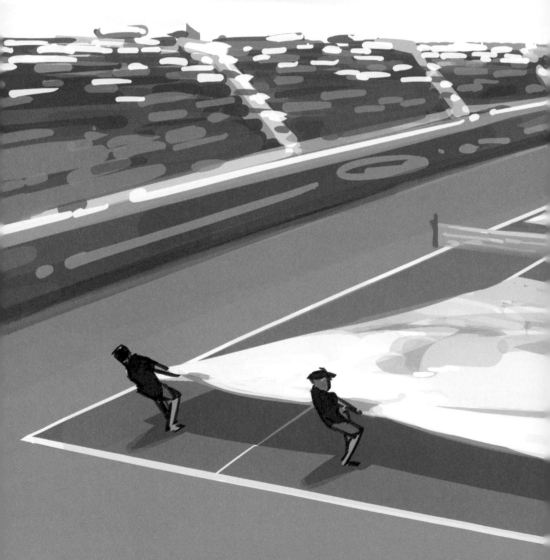

Just before the tournament starts,
workers called groundskeepers
uncover the courts.
Now you can see the courts! They are
blue with white lines. A net runs
across the middle of the court.

Players stand on opposite sides of the net and try to hit the ball back and forth over it.
They have to make sure the ball lands inside the white lines.

If it lands outside the white lines, it is called out of bounds. The players also have to hit the ball back over the net before it bounces twice on their side of the court.

Points in tennis are won in a lot of different ways.
If a player misses hitting the ball with his or her racket, the other player wins points.
If a player can't hit the ball over the net, the other player gets points.

If the ball bounces more than once
or lands outside the lines, players
win points.
My job is to get the ball off
the court after every point.

Keeping score in tennis is very
different from regular counting.
Players with zero points in a game
are said to have "love."

When someone wins one point, they
have fifteen. Two points make thirty.
And three points is forty.
Players win a game when they get
four points, but they also need to have
two more points than their opponent.

Now I'm going to help Donna warm up
for her match.
She wants to practice her serve.
That's how each point begins.
She stands behind the baseline,
throws the ball high into the air,
and hits it hard over the net with
her racket.

I hit the ball back before it bounces more than once on the court.
She also practices her forehand, backhand, and volley.
Forehand is when a player swings the racket from their side, and the palm of their hand faces forward.

For backhand, players swing their arms across their body with the back of their hand facing forward. And a volley is hitting the ball before it bounces on the court at all.

It looks like the tournament is about to begin! Mark, the chair umpire, climbs up to his high seat near the net, right outside the white lines.
His job is to keep score and make sure the players follow the rules.

Other workers, called line judges,
help the chair umpire know if the
ball was in or out of bounds.
Balls that land on the line in
tennis are considered in.

The fans are all in their seats.
Mark uses a microphone
to say the names of the players
competing today.
I get into position at the net,
ready to get the ball after each point.

It's Donna's serve. She tosses the ball into the air and hits it over the net.

The match has begun!

TEN COOL FACTS ABOUT TENNIS

1. Nearly eighty million people play tennis in 210 countries around the world.

2. Lawn tennis was invented in 1873 in Wales, a part of Great Britain, by Major Walter Clopton Wingfield.

3. The US Open tennis tournament got its start as an expansion of the US National Championship, which began in 1881.

4. The International Tennis Hall of Fame is a museum that honors the most important people in tennis history. It is located in Newport, Rhode Island.

5. The four biggest tennis tournaments in the world are called Majors.
The four Majors are:
• Wimbledon, played in London, England
• The French Open, played in Paris, France
• The US Open, played in New York City, United States
• The Australian Open, played in Melbourne, Australia
When one player wins all four of these tournaments in the same calendar season, it is called a Grand Slam.

6. Most tennis balls used to be white or black. Yellow tennis balls were first used in 1972 because they were easier for fans to see.

7. Tennis courts used to be shaped like an hourglass. That means they were narrow near the net but wider on the baselines. Now all tennis courts are rectangles.

8. Table tennis (also known as Ping-Pong) was invented as a way to play tennis indoors during bad weather.

9. The longest professional tennis match lasted eleven hours and five minutes. The 2010 match between Nicolas Mahut and John Isner was so long that it spread over three days.

10. Tennis was part of the first modern Olympics in 1896. It was removed in 1925, then returned in 1988.

EVEN MORE FACTS!

1. Martina Hingis was the youngest person in the Open Era to win the singles competition in one of the world's four major tennis tournaments. She won the 1997 Australian Open at sixteen years, 177 days old. She won the Junior French Open at age twelve!

2. Serena Williams has won the most Major tournaments during the Open Era. Through 2019 she won twenty-three Major singles titles.

3. Serena and her sister Venus Williams each won Olympic gold medals for singles and three gold medals together in doubles.

4. Switzerland honored men's champion Roger Federer by putting his picture on a postage stamp.

5. The Davis Cup is an international tournament for men's teams from more than one hundred countries. The winning country of the Davis Cup is considered the World Championship team. The women's version of the Davis Cup is called the Fed Cup.

6. The first time tennis appeared on television was in 1937. It was a match held in the town of Rye, New York, and it was seen on the NBC network.

7. Every player at Wimbledon must wear white clothes to play. Other colors are allowed at every other tournament.

8. The fastest tennis serve ever recorded was 163 miles per hour. That is faster than the fastest train in the United States.